WAY OF THE RAVEN

IMPACT WEAPONS COMBATIVES VOL.2

INTERMEDIATE TACTICAL BATON

BY

FERNAN VARGAS, MASTER AT ARMS

WAY OF THE RAVEN

IMPACT WEAPONS COMBATIVES SYSTEM
TACTICAL BATON VOLUME TWO

BY
Fernan Vargas

WAY OF THE RAVEN

IMPACT WEAPONS COMBATIVES SYSTEM

TACTICAL BATON VOLUME TWO

First Printing 2017

Raven Tactical International

Chicago, Illinois USA

www.RavenTactical.com

www.TheRavenTribe.com

www.FernanVargas.com

Speak softly and carry a big stick; you will go far.

-Theodore Roosevelt

TABLE OF CONTENTS

SAFETY & USE OF FORCE

SAFETY IN TRAINING

Safety should be the paramount consideration during any training activity. We train so that we can protect ourselves and not get hurt. Why then would we allow being hurt in training? It is the responsibility of the instructor and all class participants to ensure the safety of all. All participants in a training activity should be led through a proper warm up and stretching routine before class begins.

SAFETY EQUIPMENT

Officers should also use appropriate safety equipment for all training sessions. Equipment that should be used includes:

- -Athletic Cup
- -Athletic Mouth Piece
- -Safety head gear
- -Forearm shields
- -Safety Goggles
- -Safety Gloves

SAFETY TRAINING WEAPONS

Officers should also use safe training weapons. A variety of training blades should be used from rubber to aluminum trainers. Dulled Live blades are inappropriate for anything but solo training purposes. NO LIVE WEAPONS SHOULD EVER BE ALLOWED IN THE TRAINING AREA. A good friend of mine was working in a seminar with another instructor. The Instructor drew his blade and cut my friend across the inside of his forearm as part of his demo. The only problem is that he drew his live blade and not a trainer. Luckily a few stitches were all that were needed that day. I shudder to think what would have happened if the instructor would have been demonstrating a neck cut?

OTHER CONSIDERATIONS

-Training should be conducted in reasonable proximity of emergency medical care

-Training should be conducted in a designated training area with adequate flooring, padding and ventilation.

"When we are honorable in the small things each day, we eventually become honorable in all things in life."

— Tom Hackett

SAMPLE FORCE CONTINUUM

SUBJECT ACTION	OFFICER RESPONSE
Cooperation	**Verbal Commands**
Passive Resistance	**Escort Control**
Active Resistance	**Control & Compliance Holds**
Assault Which Can Result in Bodily Harm	**Defensive Tactics/Mechanical Controls/Less Lethal Weapons**
Assault Which Can Result In Serious Bodily Harm or Death	**Deadly Force**

**The use of force continuum presented is a general model based on common U.S. use of force guidelines. The continuum presented is for illustrative purposes only.*

FORCE CONTINUUM

The force continuum is a conceptual tool which exists to aid Officers in determining what level of force is required and justified in controlling the actions of an assailant. Verbal commands, escort techniques, mechanical controls, and deadly force are all options which are available to an Officer depending upon the assailant's actions. Force escalation must cease when the assailant complies with the commands of the Officer, and/or the situation is controlled by the Officer. The model presented bellow consists of five levels. Physical defensive tactics are appropriate from levels three to five.

Level One: The assailant cooperates with the Officer's verbal commands. Physical actions are not required.

Level Two: The assailant is unresponsive to verbal commands. Assailant cooperation however is achieved with escort techniques.

Level Three: The assailant actively resists the Officer's attempts to control without being assault. Compliance and control holds as well as pain compliance techniques are appropriate actions at this time.

Level Four: The assailant assaults an Officer or another person with actions which are likely to cause bodily harm. Appropriate action would include mechanical controls or defensive tactics such as stunning techniques. Impact and chemical weapons may be appropriate at this level.

Level Five: The assailant assaults an Officer or another person with actions which are likely to cause serious bodily harm or death if not stopped immediately. Appropriate Officer action would include deadly force through mechanical controls, Impact weapons or firearms. Deadly force should be considered only when lesser means have been exhausted, are unavailable or cannot be reasonably employed.

DECISION OF FORCE

When making the decision to use force an Officer should use the minimal amount of "Reasonable" force necessary to safely control the situation at hand. When using deadly force for self defense an Officer must be prepared to articulate and justify their use of a force.

"Reasonable force" can be defined: *force that is not excessive and is the least amount of force that will permit safe control of the situation while still maintaining a level of safety for himself or herself and the public.*

An Officer is justified in the use of force when they reasonably believe it to be necessary to defend themselves or another from bodily harm and have no avenue for reasonable escape.

Escalation and de-escalation of resistance and response may occur without going through each successive level. The Officer has the option to escalate or disengage, repeat the technique, or escalate to any level at any time. However, the Officer will need to justify any response to resistance. If the Officer skips levels, he or she must explain why it was necessary to do so.

TOTALITY OF CIRCUMSTANCES

Totality of circumstances refers to all facts and circumstances known to the Officer at the time. The totality of circumstances includes consideration of the assailant's form of resistance, all reasonably perceived factors that may have an effect on the situation, and the response options available to the Officer.

SAMPLE FACTORS MAY INCLUDE THE FOLLOWING:

- Severity of the assault or battery
- Assailant is an immediate threat
- Assailant's mental or psychiatric history, if known to the Officer
- Assailant's violent history, if known to the Officer
- Assailant's combative skills
- Assailant's access to weapons
- Innocent bystanders who could be harmed
- Number of assailant's vs. number of Officers
- Duration of confrontation
- Assailant's size, age, weight, and physical condition
- The Officer's size, age, weight, physical condition, and defensive tactics expertise

- Environmental factors, such as physical terrain, weather conditions, etc.

In all cases where your assessment and decision are questioned you may need to demonstrate the following:

- That you felt physically threatened by and in danger from the suspect, i.e. that the suspect's behavior (body language/ words / actions) were aggressive and threatening;

- That you used force as a last resort, and that you used the reasonable amount;

- That you stopped using force once you had the suspect and the situation under control.

- That the Officer has exhausted all reasonable efforts to escape the situation.

ABOUT THE SYSTEM

ABOUT THE SYSTEM

The program is a multi-level program which trains individuals on a variety of impact weapons. The program teaches the Mini-baton, the Telescopic Baton, Riot Baton, Side Handle baton and more. This manual will specifically address the use of the Telescopic Baton for Peacekeeping personnel. While the material here is easily adapted to civilian or battlefield use, it is primarily designed with the law enforcement community in mind and the use of force concerns often presented to police personnel.

The Program is not a stick fighting martial art such as Kali or Hanbo-Jutsu. The program is designed to be completed in a short period of time. The Program is meant to impart the student with "SURVIVAL ESSENTIALS". That is a minimum effective proficiency for self protection. This is not to say that the program is lacking in fact the program can be as functional and "Advanced" as the student wished it to be. Remember that "Advanced Material is the basics done well". Properly drilled and trained over time, this program can offer anyone a highly effective and reliable skill set for the use of the Telescopic Baton.

This program draws from numerous sources, including a variety of Police Baton methods, military baton methods, and select tactics from Stick Fighting Martial Arts or "Martial Baton Methods".

HOW SHOULD THIS BOOK BE USED?

This book is primarily for the purpose of entertainment and information. There are those however who may wish to use it to train from. The book is not meant to be a training guide without the guidance of a qualified instructor. If anyone is interested in using the book as a training guide please contact me. I will connect you to a qualified instructor to guide you, or I will assist you myself.

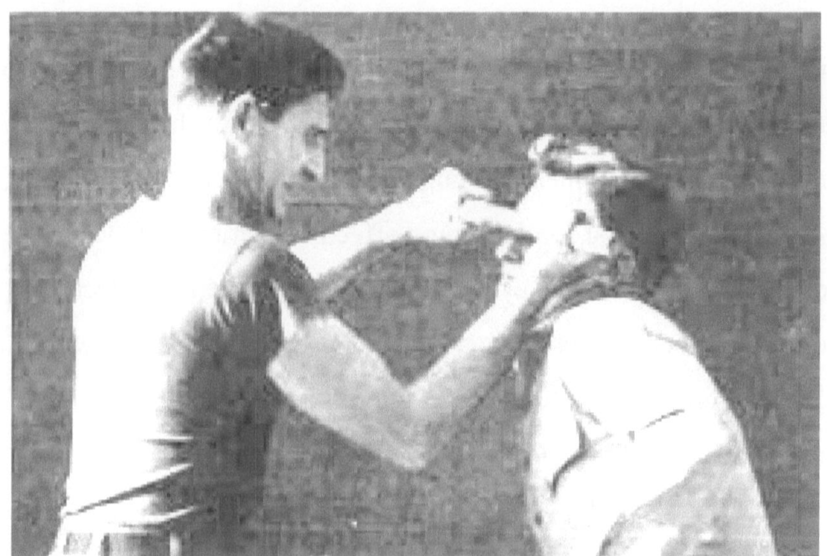

OBSTRUCTED ATTACK SOLUTIONS

OBSTRUCTED ATTACK SOLUTIONS

There will be times when the Officer is attempting to complete and attack and the subject creates an obstruction to this attack. The Officer has several ways to properly address the obstructed attack. They include:

-Pulling the obstructing limb
-Pushing the obstructed limb
-Taking a secondary line of attack

OBSTRUCTED ATTACK SOLUTION: THE PULL

1. The assailant blocks and obstructs the Officer's initial attack.
2. The Officer uses his free hand to pull the obstruction away
3. The Officer is then free to counter attack if needed.

OBSTRUCTED ATTACK SOLUTION: THE PUSH

1. The assailant blocks and obstructs the Officer's initial attack.
2. The Officer uses his free hand to push the obstruction away
3. The Officer is then free to counter attack if needed.

OBSTRUCTED ATTACK SOLUTION: SECONDARY LINES

1. The assailant blocks and obstructs the Officer's initial attack.
2. The Officer pulls his initial attack away from the obstruction and finds an unobstructed path on which to complete the attack.
3. The Officer is then free to counter attack if needed.

DRILLS & EXERCISES

FUNCTIONAL DRILLS

Our System uses a variety of simple drills to enhance the officer's ability to successfully deal with a weapon assault. The drills are designed to emphasize specific components which give the officer ample time to develop the appropriate attributes needed to use the skills successfully. While most of the drills in the system are easy to learn and use, regular practice is still recommended. It is also recommended that each component be practiced as individual skill-sets before putting them together to create a complete response.

DEFLECT & DISENGAGE DRILL

For this drill two partners will pair up. One will be the attacker and the other will be the defender. The partners will begin by standing 7-21 feet from each other. The attacker will then feed the defender an attack. The defender will attempt to move off line and avoid the attack, using their baton to deflect and redirect the incoming attack. Once the attack is deflected the defender should attempt to disengage and get out of measure. The attacker will continue to attack the defender from various angles. The attacks can be predetermined and then gradually become random. The speed and intensity of the attacks can also be gradually increased.

DEFLECT & ENGAGE DRILL

For this drill two partners will pair up. One will be the attacker and the other will be the defender. The partners will begin by standing 7 feet or less from each other. Where the goal in the previous drill was to avoid and separate from the attacker, the goal of this drill is to avoid the initial attack and close the distance to counter attack. The attacker will continue to attack the defender from various angles. The attacks can be predetermined and then gradually become random. The speed and intensity of the attacks can also be gradually increased.

SPONTANEOUS DEFENSE DRILL

To perform this drill, multiple subjects will surround and circle the officer. The subjects will take turns randomly attacking the officer. The attacks will be staggered so the officer can not time the attacks. The officer should defend and counter attack this drill will assist the officer in inoculating themselves to ambush or surprise attacks.

MEET & FOLLOW THE FORCE

One excellent drill for developing hand-eye coordination, timing and reaction time is the Meet & Follow Force Drill. As the assailant Attacks the Officer, the Officer will meet the incoming attack with his weapon, coming to the inside of the opponent's arc of power. Meeting the force is most often a proactive way of addressing an incoming attack.

FOLLOW THE FORCE DRILL SERIES

As the assailant Attacks the Officer , the Officer is not prepared and is not quick enough to meet the incoming attack with his weapon, coming to the inside of the opponents arc of power. The Officer then uses body movement to avoid thc attack and then address the attack on the "back end" by following the attack. Following the force is a most often a Reactive way of addressing an incoming attack.

MEET THE FORCE/FOLLOW THE FORCE ADD ONS

Once the Officer has mastered these two basic drills the Officer can build upon them in the following ways. Once the Officer addresses the initial attack the Officer will adjust their position and then execute one of the following. `1

DOWNWARD DIAGONAL ATTACKS

Once the Officer has addressed the initial attack, the Officer will execute forehand downward diagonal attack followed by a back hand downward diagonal attack.

UPWARD DIAGONAL ATTACKS

Once the Officer has addressed the initial attack, the Officer will execute forehand upward diagonal attack followed by a back hand upward diagonal attack.

HORIZONTAL ATTACKS

Once the Officer has addressed the initial attack, the Officer will execute forehand horizontal attack followed by a back hand horizontal attack.

THRUSTING ATTACKS

Once the Officer has addressed the initial attack, the Officer will execute two thrusting attacks.

HIT AND GRAB DRILL

In this drill the officer will practice bringing the live hand into play. The goal of the drill is to develop the officer's ability to defend with the baton and immediately use the live hand to seize the enemy's arm either at the wrist or the forearm. This drill can be performed in a few different ways. To begin the Enemy will feed the officer the series of angles from any of the established patterns or templates. The enemy can also opt to feed angles randomly. The officer in response will either meet the enemy's force or follow it, defending with the baton by either hitting the enemy's arm or using a block. Once the Officer has successfully defended the initial attack they will then reach in with the live hand and seize the enemy's arm at the forearm or wrist. The officer can make the seizure from either the inside or the outside of the enemy's arm. The better the grip of the Officer the more effective the skill will be in combat.

SPONTANEOUS DEFENSE DRILL

To perform this drill, multiple subjects will surround and circle the Officer. The subjects will take turns randomly attacking the Officer. The attacks will be staggered so the Officer can not time the attacks. The Officer should use techniques and concepts taught in the course to address the attacks. This drill will assist the Officer in inoculating themselves to ambush or surprise attacks.

3-2-1 DRILL

In this drill, one partner will attack and freeze for 3 seconds. In those three seconds the other partner should counter and attack in a spontaneous fashion. At the end of the three seconds the attacking partner will then break away and attack again. The purpose of this drill is to allow the Officer to acquire target acquisition skills, proper coordination, attack sequencing and timing. Once the Officer feels comfortable with 3 seconds, the drill should drop down to 2 seconds and finally one second. This progression will lead the Officer to real time sparring and scenarios by gradually building the skill level needed for a more realistic tempo in training.

IMPAIRMENT DRILLS

In the chaos of combat there is no guarantee of ideal conditions. If an officer has never faced combat or contest under stress or duress they may find themselves in for a rude awakening. While I do not advocate that an officer go out and seek the lessons of true combat I do advocate the simulation of conditions they may find in such. There are several simple things that the Officer can do to simulate these conditions. The more the Officer is exposed to these impairments the better prepared they will be to fight through them. Just as a block or evasion is trained as a proper response to an attack, the Officer will train their bodies to respond correctly when faced with injury or stress.

STROBE LIGHT DRILL

One of the best drills I ever learned was given to me by Grand Master Gus Michalik. G.M. Gus shared with me the wonders of strobe light training and sparring. A strobe light gives the visual illusion of slow motion, something often reported as an effect of high stress encounters. A strobe light can also be very disorienting. Both of these conditions are perfect for taking an officer out of their comfort zone. Officers who train under the strobe light will be able to experience a very chaotic environment which in many ways mimics the realities of combat stress. By training under these conditions the Officer can become familiar with the feeling of disorientation and therefore learn to perform in less than ideal conditions. For this drill I recommend an industrial strobe light. I have rented them from lighting companies in the past for about $50.00 a day. The small ones you can buy at the novelty store usually won't be able to give you the effect you need, as they don't flash as powerfully or frequently.

APACHE VISIBILITY TRAINING

My friend and Apache Battle Tactics instructor Snake Blocker has a panache for training drills. He is one of the best sources I have found for interesting training drills. Snake has made a career of collecting and cataloging traditional Apache games and drills which relate directly to combat training. Here are a few of my favorite drills which Snake has shared with me. Taking a page out of the Apache play book, Officers can practice all of their drills, training sets and sparring in a variety of lighting conditions. The goal is to accustom the Officer to the various lighting conditions which they may encounter. The three conditions under which the Officer should train are:

STAGE ONE: DAY LIGHT/FULL LIGHT:
PHOTOPIC VISION

Photopic visual conditions allow for high visual acuity and color perception. Under these conditions light is processed by the cones of the eyes.

STAGE TWO: MID LIGHT:
MESOPIC VISION

Mesopic vision is used in low light conditions which are not totally dark. In the mesopic range the eyes use both the cones and rods to process light. A common example of mesopic conditions would be a city street at night lit by street lights and other ambient light. These lighting conditions are very common to a variety of assault scenarios. It is crucial for an officer to practice their art under these conditions. While it is very possible to be robbed or assaulted in the light of day, many criminals will choose to mask their acts at night.

STAGE THREE: LOW LIGHT/NO LIGHT: SCOTOPIC VISION

Under scotopic visual conditions the eyes process light exclusively with the rods. Scotopic visual conditions will range from very low light to no light at all. Color discrimination is virtually non-existent under these conditions and visual acuity is very low. Officers will find these conditions to be the most challenging in training. Because vision is so impaired under these conditions extra attention to safety in training must be a consideration.

THE CIRCLE OF DEATH

To perform this drill, multiple assailants will surround and circle the Officer. The assailants will take turns randomly attacking the Officer. The attacks will be staggered so the Officer can not time the attacks. This drill will assist the Officer in inoculating themselves to ambush or surprise attacks.

BLURRY VISION

If the Officer is using eye wear (as they always should) a swipe of lip balm across the lenses of their goggles can be used to impair vision. Also see the section on Drills and visual concepts in this book for further ideas on how to train the vision for all combat conditions.

DIZZINESS

Remember when you were 5 yrs old and would spin around until you were dizzy? Try the same trick before a sparring session. The dizziness can mimic the impaired equilibrium you may face if you took a good shot to the head or were loosing blood from a wound.

LOSS OF LIMB

A gnarled and damaged limb can definitely put a cramp in your style. Have you trained for it? If not you should start now. It is as easy as putting one hand in your pocket or behind your back. Switch to your off hand or splint your leg to simulate a damaged one. As mentioned in previous chapters a little oil on the hand can train the Officer to hold onto a baton with a blood soaked hand. All of these simple tricks can help the Officer learn how to adapt to an injured body.

SPARRING

In my humble opinion no drill is more useful and yet more incorrectly used than sparring. Yes, sparring is a drill. It is not a match. The difference is very clear. In a match both parties are intent on besting the other, the purpose is a test of skill. In a sparring drill the purpose is training a skill, not testing it. If you are sparring without a specific goal, and without pre and post sparring instruction, then you are not sparring. You are having a match. While many take this approach in training I feel it is a mistake. A student could match 1000 times a day and still never see improvement absent instruction.

Presented here are a few of my favorite sparring variations. I encourage all readers to expand and modify the variations presented. I also encourage the reader to innovate their own variations. Remember, sparring is a goal oriented drill. All sparring should have clear parameters and goals. These should be monitored closely by the instructor or senior practitioner present.

ISOLATION SPARRING

In "isolation sparring" the Officer will focus on one particular technique or tactic. An officer may for example dedicate their sparring session to the working of thrusting techniques. The sparring partner will be free to feed any techniques they like but the Officer will focus on answering those attacks with thrusting techniques. Attacks, foot work, defenses, all can be used in a variety of isolation sparring sessions to advance the Officers skill.

IMPAIRMENT SPARRING

In the chaos of combat there is no guarantee of ideal conditions. If an officer has never faced combat or contest under stress or duress they may find themselves in for a rude awakening. While I do not advocate that an officer go out and seek the lessons of true combat I do advocate the simulation of conditions they may find in such. There are several simple things that the Officer can do to simulate these conditions. The more the Officer is exposed to these impairments the better prepared they will be to fight through them. Just as a block or evasion is trained as a proper response to an attack, the Officer will train their bodies to respond correctly when faced with injury or stress.

VISUAL

If the Officer is using eye wear (as they always should) a swipe of lip balm across the lenses of their goggles can be used to impair vision. Also see the section on Drills and visual concepts in this book for further ideas on how to train the vision for all combat conditions.

DIZZINESS

Remember when you were 5 yrs old and would spin around until you were dizzy? Try the same trick before a sparring session. The dizziness can mimic the impaired equilibrium you may face if you took a good shot to the head or were loosing blood from a wound.

LOSS OF LIMB

A gnarled and damaged limb can definitely put a cramp in your style. Have you trained for it? If not you should start now. It is as easy as putting one hand in your pocket or behind your back. Switch to your off hand or splint your leg to simulate a damaged one. As mentioned in previous chapters a little oil on the hand can train the Officer to hold onto a baton with a blood soaked hand. All of these simple tricks can help the Officer learn how to adapt to an injured body.

COMBAT STRESS

Muscles tighten, breath is labored, and your focus is challenged. These are just a few of the things that you can expect to experience under the stressful conditions of combat. When the fight or flight response is triggered the body draws blood from the extremities to the core and vital organs. Do you know what else triggers these changes? COLD. A little sparring out doors in the winter or a bucket of ice cold water in the summer is all that you need to experience these feelings.

PHONE BOOTH SPARRING

While I love the long range game, and would choose it 9 out of 10 times if given the option, we must train for the extreme close quarter engagement as well. What if you're assaulted between parked cars in a parking lot, in a tight corridor or in an elevator? To train this range, use tape on the floor to create a small box and spar inside of it. Doing so will force you to work different skills such as your checking hands, trapping and more.

MIXED WEAPONS SPARRING

Baton VS empty hand is one thing but baton VS chain, baseball bat, or folding chair is another. The Officer should take time to partake in mixed weapon sparring sessions. Doing so will prepare the Officer for the differences in reach, speed, and many other variable presented by different weapons.

TOTAL BODY SPARRING

Total body sparring will see the Officer engage in sparring that involves not only their baton but their other weapons as well, hands feet, elbows, etc. In this sparring drill the Officer will learn to incorporate strikes and blows as well as the attacks of their baton.

LETHAL FORCE COMBATIVES

LETHAL FORCE COMBATIVES

There are times when an Officer may need to use their baton as a lethal force tool in defense of their lives or the life of another. Should an Officer find themselves at this threat level, they may use the following techniques.

NOTE, THE FOLLOWING TECHNIQUES ARE LIKELY TO CAUSE GREAT BODILY HARM OR DEATH. THE TECHNIQUES SHOULD NOT BE USED UNDER ANY CIRCUMSTANCES UNLESS THE OFFICER STRONGLY BELIEVES THAT THEIR LIFE OR THE LIFE OF ANOTHER INDIVIDUAL IS IN DANGER AND ALL OTHER REASONABLE OPTIONS HAVE BEEN EXHUSTED.

In the RTI Baton Method the following techniques are taught as Techniques which are appropriate to apply during a lethal force encounter.

- LF Striking
- Chokes
- Take Downs
- Ground Defense
- Weapon Retention

BATON CONTROL HOLDS & LETHAL FORCE

The Raven Method Tactical Baton System does NOT advocate the use of the baton as a control device for less lethal force encounters. The reason for this is that in order to apply the techniques the Officer must apply stress to the joints, and other areas such as the spine, or kidneys. Even though the Officer is applying slow direct pressure and not impact force, the effected areas of the subject's body are sensitive and the Officer can not ensure that the application of the technique will be 100% safe for the subject. Applying potentially lethal force to a resisting subject who is not combative is unacceptable. Also it is unlikely that an Officer will apply a control hold in a combative situation. Officer interviews suggest that even Officer's who are trained to execute control holds will rarely do so under stress, and instead using a striking tool set. Training Officer's to perform control holds also creates an expectation that they should implement this tactic before using the baton to strike/ stun. This is a dangerous burden to place on Officer's, as the situation may warrant striking techniques rather than control holds. Officer should not be held to a graduated progression if it is at the cost of their own safety.

LETHAL FORCE STRIKING TECHNIQUES

Officers will rely on the striking techniques in their tool box as their primary lethal force options with the baton. Officers should carefully study the lethal force targets on the body in order to 1. Minimize damage and liability when not using lethal force, and 2. To be able to effectively target a lethal force target in a life or death situation.

LEVEL III: LETHAL FORCE

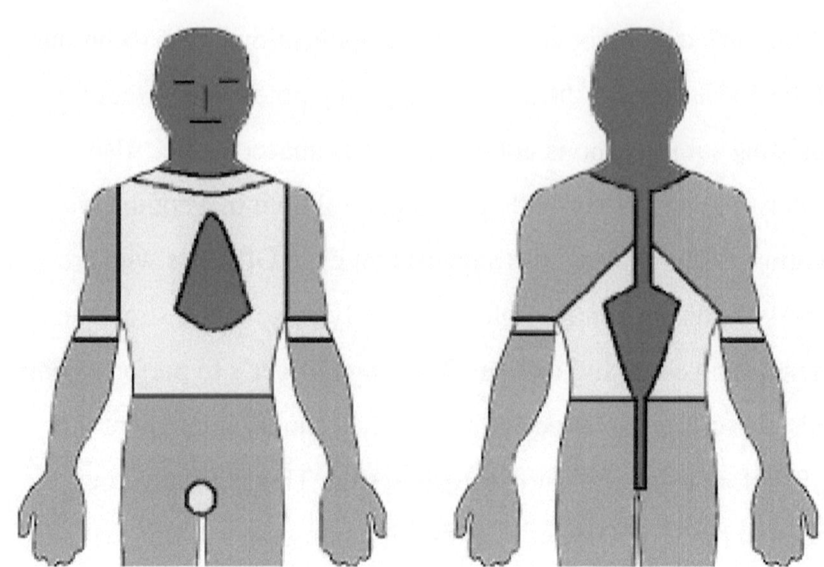

LEVEL III: LETHAL FORCE

Level Three targets are last resort lethal force targets. An office should never attempt a stun to these targets unless the Officer fears that the subject posses a threat of death or seriously injure to the Officer or another.

Spine	Ear	Bridge of Nose	Eyes
Kidney	Throat	Lower Jaw	Tail Bone
Solar Plexus	Neck	Temple	Upper Jaw
Base of Neck	Groin		

UPWARD SMASH

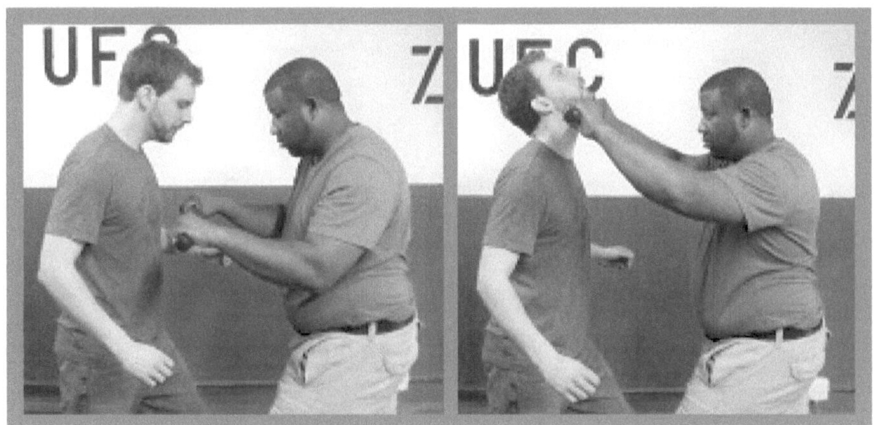

To execute the upward smash the Officer assumes the two handed guard. The Officer will hold the baton under the desired target and then rapidly lift upwards, moving at the elbow and shoulder to strike the target with the middle shaft of the baton.

DOWNWARD SMASH

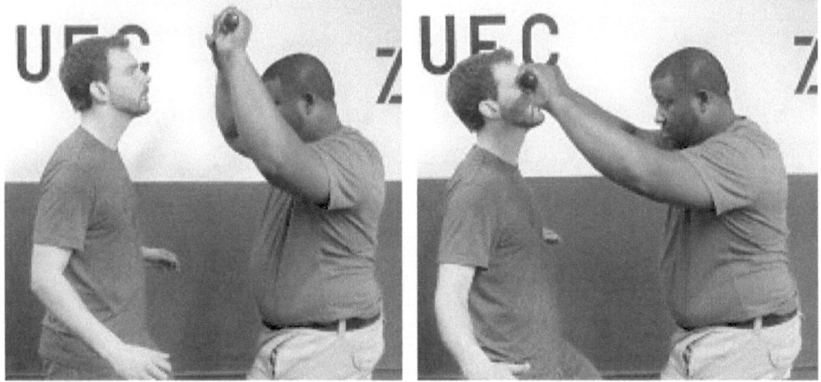

To execute the Downward smash the Officer assumes the two handed guard. The Officer will hold the baton above the desired target and then rapidly lift upwards, moving at the elbow and shoulder to strike the target with the middle shaft of the baton.

BATON CHOKES

REAR CROSS CHOKE

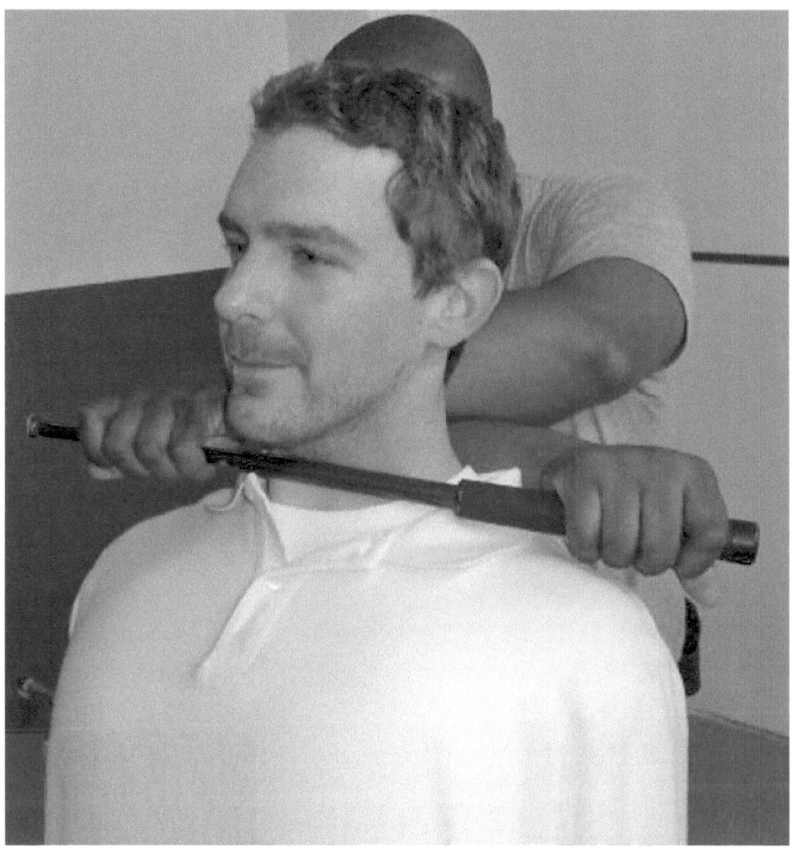

The technique is applied by holding the baton in a reverse grip. The Officer should place their wrist on the subject's neck on the same side. This will place the shaft of the baton across the subject's throat. The Officer should then cross his free hand and grip the baton shaft on the other side. The Officer should have both wrists close to the subject's neck. Once secured the Officer squeeze tight and pull his hands to his navel.

REAR CHOKE

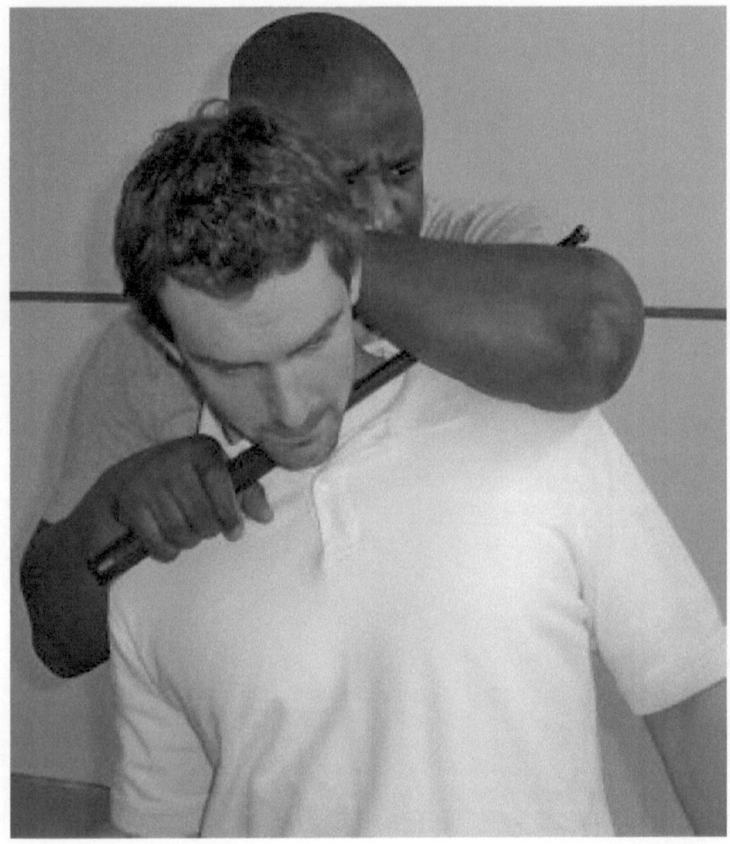

To execute the rear choke, the Officer must start by placing the baton across the subject's neck or throat. Once the baton is in place the Officer will insert their free hand and place the end shaft of the baton in the pit of the elbow of the free hand. The Officer next will place his free hand behind the subjects head at the base of the skull. The Officer now will simultaneously push the head down, while squeezing his elbows in tight to his own body and extending his lateral muscles

REAR PULLING CHOKE

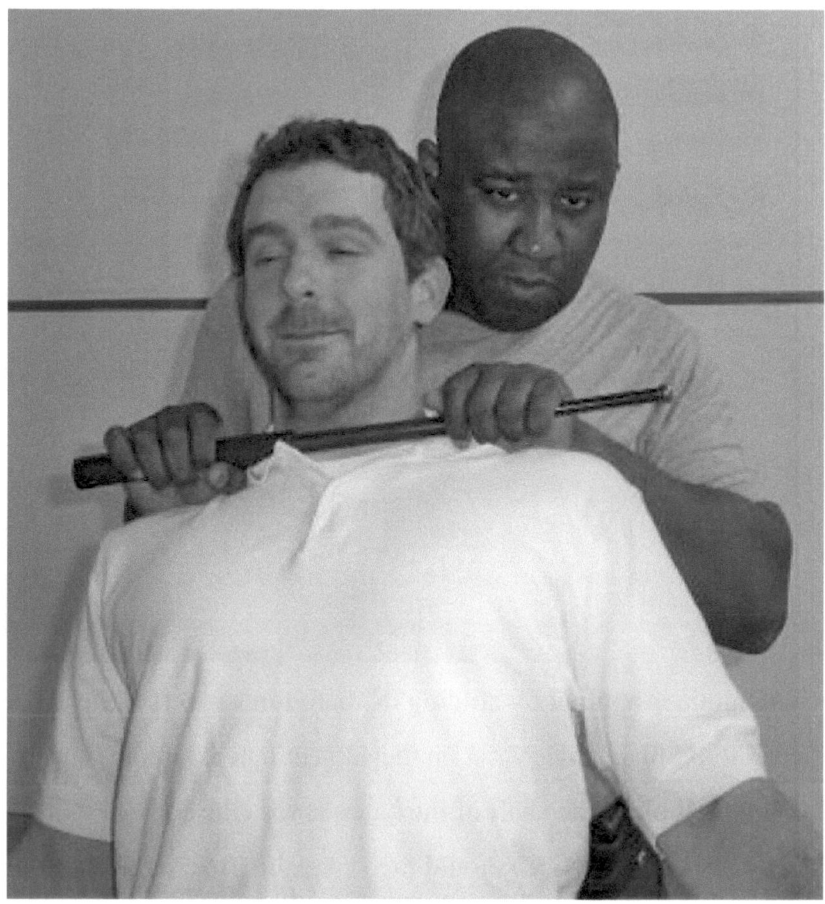

To execute the rear pulling choke, the Officer must first extend the baton across the subject's neck directly below their chin. The Officer's hands should be snug on both sides of the subject's neck. The Officer then secures the baton from both sides and pulls both hands to his own waist while stepping back to ensure the subject does not fall directly on him.

CHOKE HOLDS: FRONT CROSS CHOKE

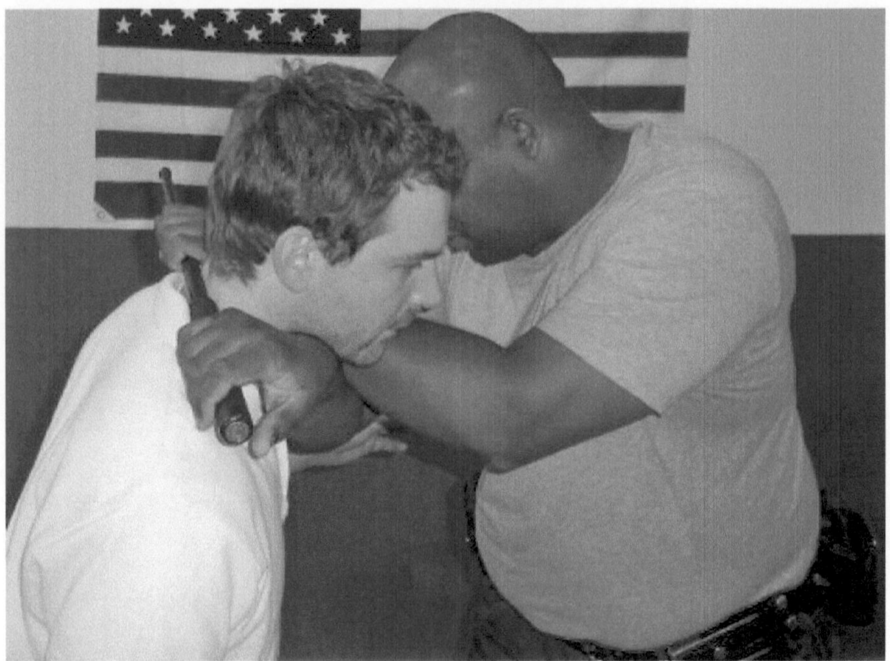

The technique is applied by holding the baton in a reverse grip. The Officer should place their wrist on the subject's neck on the same side. This will place the shaft of the baton across the back of the subject's neck. The Officer should then cross his free hand and grip the baton shaft on the other side. The Officer should have both wrists close to the subject's neck. Once secured the Officer squeeze tight and pull his hands to his navel

CHOKE HOLDS: DIAGONAL PULLING CHOKE

To execute the rear Diagonal pulling choke, the Officer must first extend the baton under the subjects arm pit and across the chest. The Officer will grip the baton on the opposite end. The Officer then secures the baton from both sides and pulls both hands to his own waist while stepping back to ensure the subject does not fall directly on him.

"It isn't enough to stand up and fight darkness. You've got to stand apart from it, too. You've got to be different from it."

-Jim Butcher

BATON TAKE DOWNS

TAKE DOWN: HIP PULL TAKE DOWN

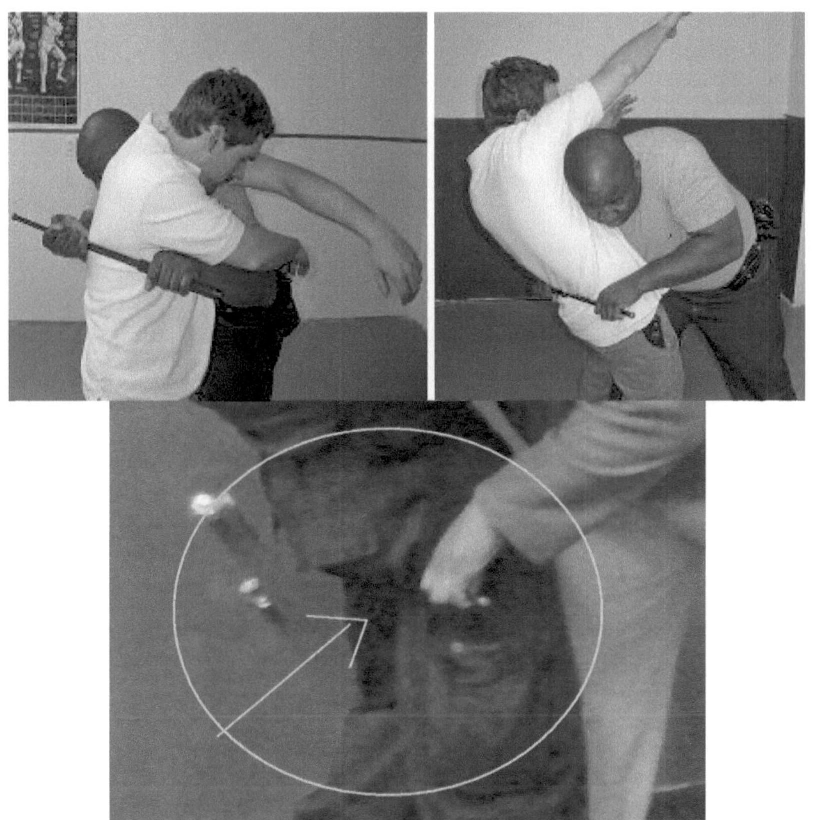

Begin by wrapping the baton around the assailants back. Lower the baton around the assailant's waist while simultaneously pulling the baton towards your own torso and pushing into the assailant with your shoulder. Make sure your head is to the outside of the assailant's body. Once the assailant begins to loose balance, release one side of the baton to release the assailant so they fall to the ground without the Officer going to the ground. A safer variation of the take down which does not go against the spine is pictured in the third photograph. Here the Officer wraps behind the subjects buttocks rather than the swell of the back. the take down is equally effective.

DOUBLE LEG TAKEDOWN

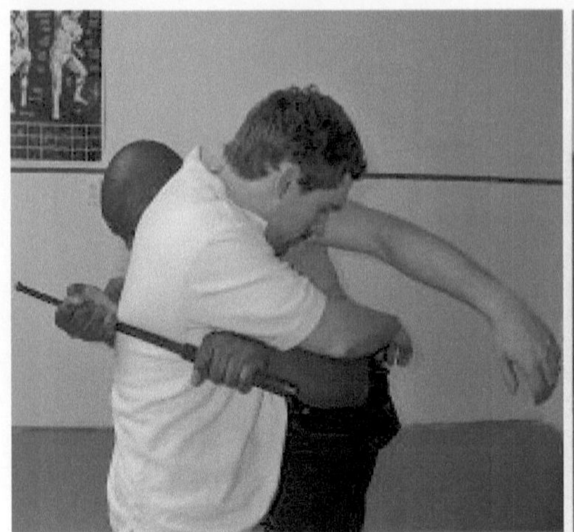

Begin by wrapping the baton around the assailants back. Lower the baton around the assailant's waist while simultaneously pulling the baton towards your own torso and pushing into the assailant with your shoulder. Make sure your head is to the outside of the assailant's body. Once the assailant begins to loose balance, Drop the baton behind their knees and continue to drive with the shoulder. Release one side of the baton to release the assailant so they fall to the ground without the Officer going to the ground.

HEAD PULL TAKE DOWN

To execute the head pull take down, the Officer must first extend the baton across back of the subject's neck. The Officer's hands should be snug on both sides of the subject's neck. The Officer then secures the baton from both sides and pulls both hands to his own waist while stepping back to ensure the subject does not fall directly on him.

"It is a good man who stands up for his friends, but an honorable man who stands up for his enemies."

-Violet Haberdasher

GROUND TECHNIQUES

GROUND APPLICATIONS

There are times when an Officer may find themselves on the ground during an altercation. If the Officer finds themselves in this position they should first seek to establish a good defensive position and then Safely make the transition back to the standing position. Officer's should practice applying all of the standing baton techniques on the on the ground as well, as they translate effectively. Some considerations must be made as well as adjustments but the overall theories and strategies are still very sound. Bellow is a series of sequences which are meant to be a small skill set. The Officer must add to this skill set through the use flexible application of the standing core techniques to ground situations. This will be best accomplished by the use of Functional training drill.

Officers should also note that Ground techniques are potentially lethal force scenarios for two reasons. 1. The Officer is in a compromised position where they are not able to properly defend themselves and 2. because in order to apply some of the ground fighting techniques the Officer must apply stress to the joints, and other areas such as the spine, or kidneys. Even though the Officer is applying slow direct pressure and not impact force, the effected areas of the subject's body are sensitive and the Officer can not ensure that the application of the technique will be 100% safe for the subject.

MOUNT DEFENSE #1

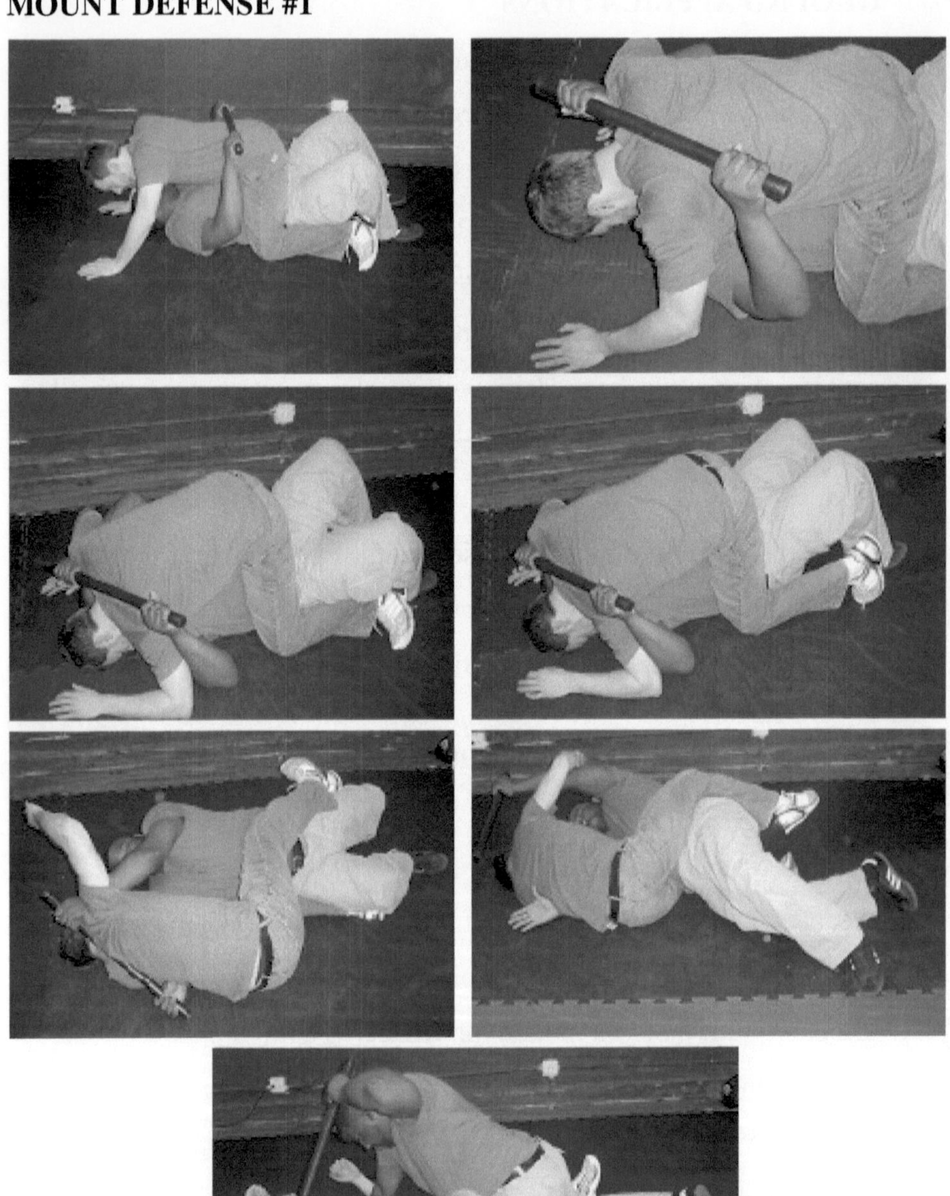

The Officer finds himself mounted by the subject. The Officer wraps the baton around the subjects back. The Officer brings the baton across the subjects shoulder. The Officer pulls the subject into him towards the ground.

The Officer now raises his hips, further putting the subject off balance. The Officer now rolls to towards the subject's trapped shoulder, rolling the subject off of the Officer. The Officer then assumes a ready position, where he can strike or disengage.

"A person less fortunate than yourself deserves the best you can give. Because of duty, and honor, and service. You understand those words? You should do your job right, and you should do it well, simply because you can, without looking for notice or reward."

-Lee child

SCISSOR SWEEP

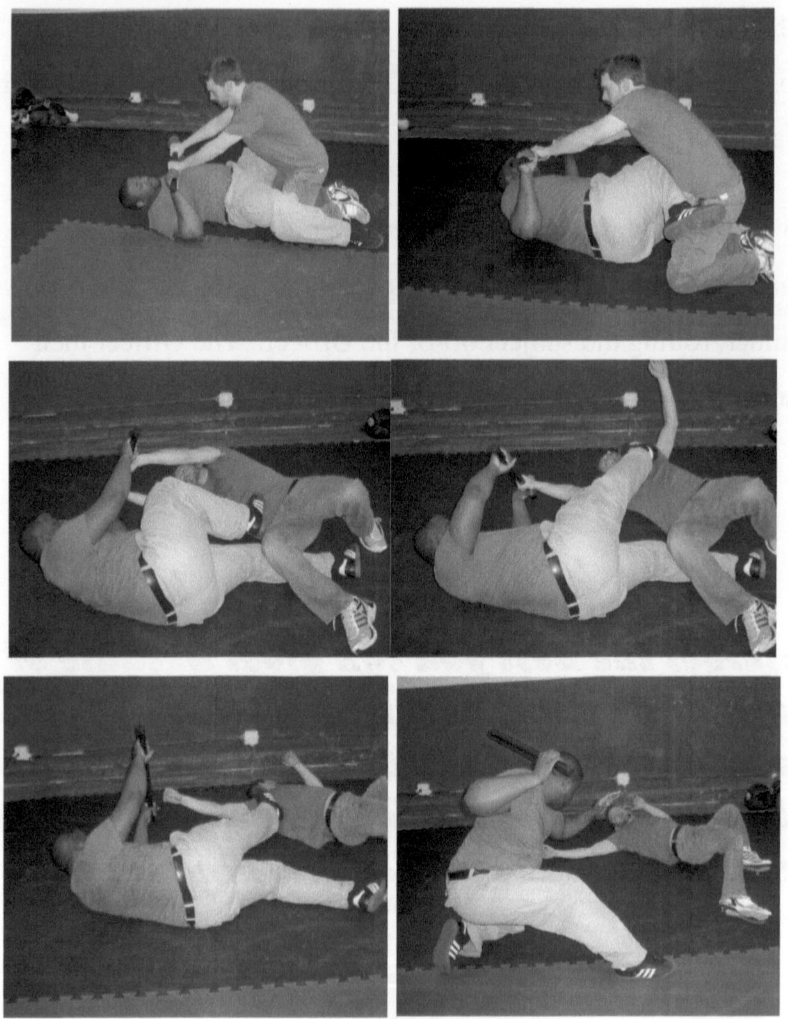

The Officer finds the subject in his guard fighting for the Officer's baton. The subject has two hands on the baton. Turn to side, and then Scissor your legs, while pulling the secured arm. Once the subject has been taken over, the Officer kicks the subjects arm to free his grip on the baton. The Officer then kicks to the other arm to free the baton entirely. The Officer now assumes a defensive stance while returning to his feet.

MOUNT DEFENSE #2

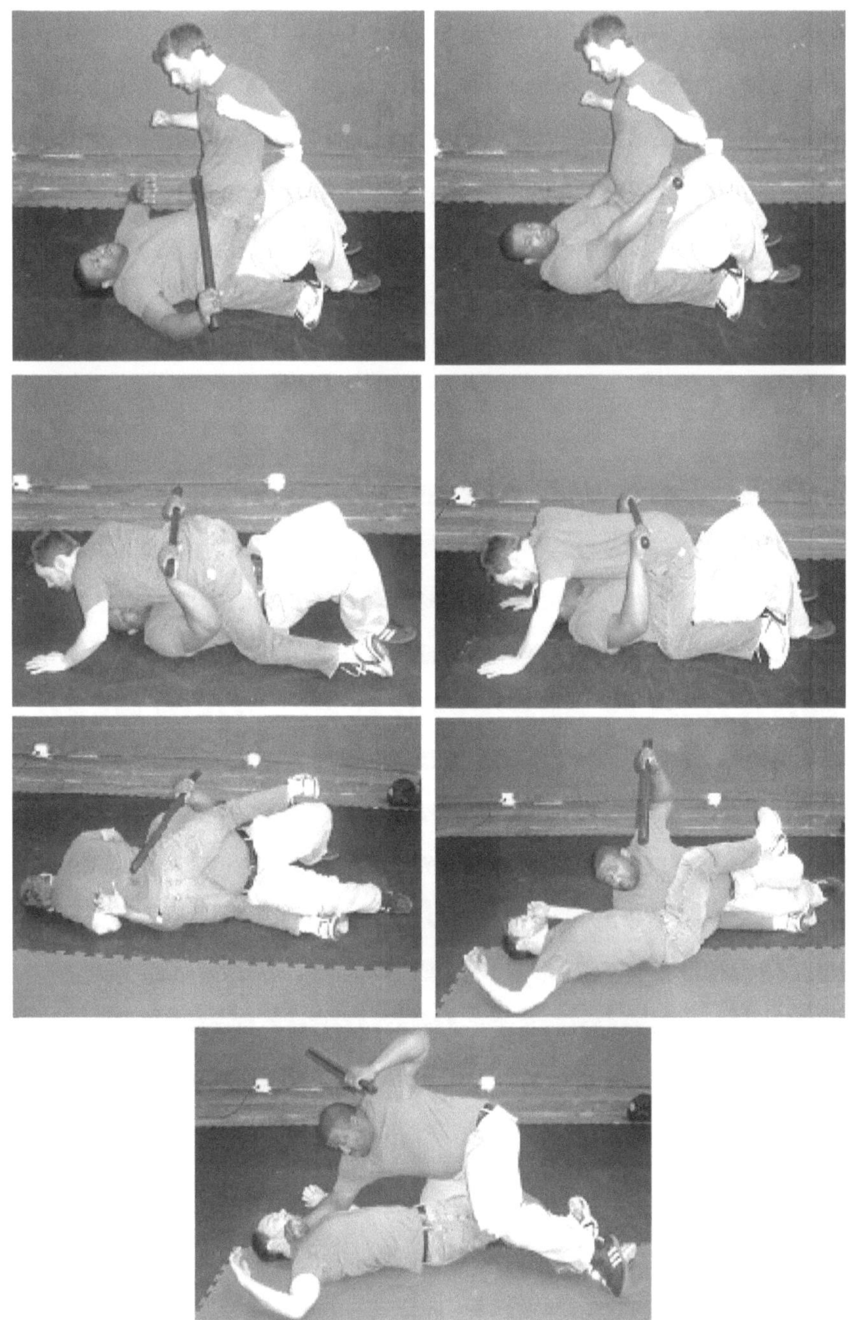

The Officer finds himself mounted by the subject. The Officer wraps the baton around the subjects back. The Officer brings the baton across the subjects shoulder. The Officer pulls the subject into him towards the ground. The Officer now raises his hips, further putting the subject off balance. The Officer now rolls to towards the subject's trapped shoulder, rolling the subject off of the Officer. The Officer then assumes a ready position, where he can strike or disengage.

"The hero acts alone, without encouragement, relying solely on conviction and his own inner resources. Shame does not discourage him; neither does obloquy. Indifferent to approval, reputation, wealth, or love, he cherishes only his personal sense of honor, which he permits no one else to judge. Guided by an inner gyroscope, he pursues his vision single-mindedly, undiscouraged by rejections, defeat, or even the prospect of imminent death."

-William Manchester

TWO HANDED ANKLE PICK:

Officer takes his baton and places it behind the assailant's ankle. The Officer will use their shoulder to apply slow and direct pressure to the thigh or shin or knee. *Note the Officer keeps his head to the outside of the subject's body. The Officer monitors the subject's legs to avoid being struck with a kick. The Officer is now ready to retreat to his feet.

DOUBLE LEG TAKE DOWN

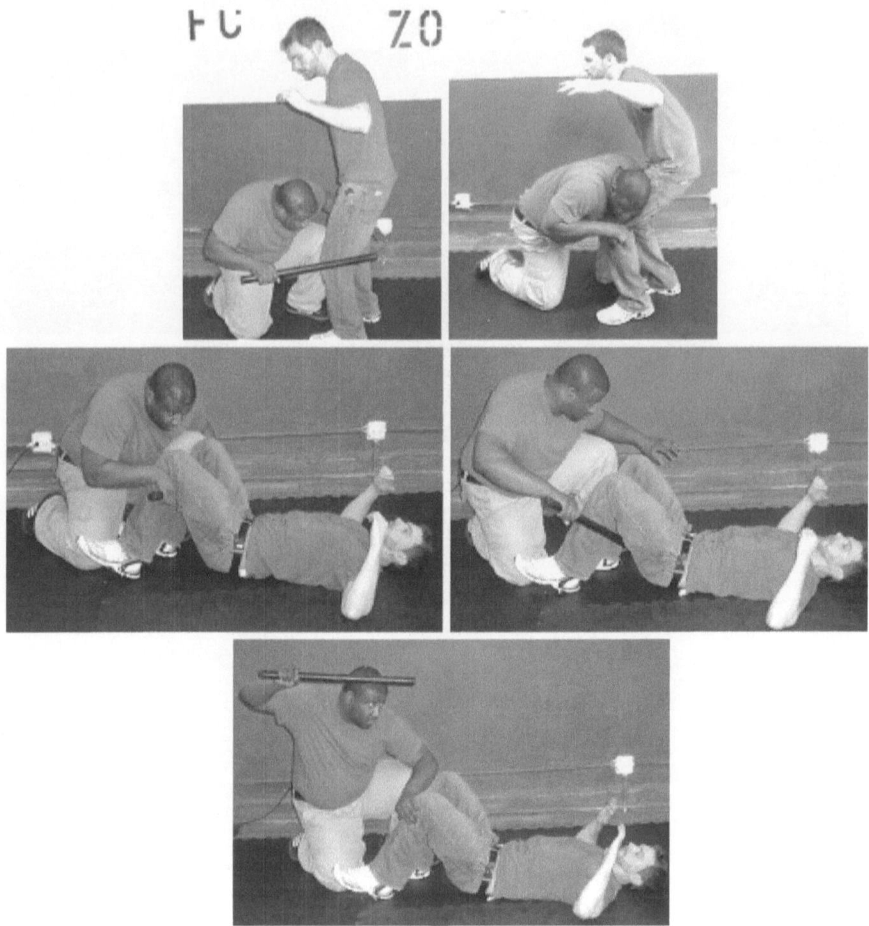

Officer takes his baton and places it behind the assailant's knees. The Officer will use their shoulder to apply slow and direct pressure to the thigh or shin or knee. *Note the Officer keeps his head to the outside of the subject's body. The Officer releases one end of the baton in order to free it from behind the subject's legs. The Officer monitors the subject's legs to avoid being struck with a kick. And is now ready to retreat to his feet.

GROUND STRIKING

All of the striking techniques in the RTI Telescopic Baton Manual are equally applicable from the various ground positions. The Thrusting strikes presented below are for illustrative purposes.

"Break every chain of mediocrity that confines you. You may have begun at a level below average, but dare to leave that side and paddle your steps to cross the river with honours."

-Israelmore Ayivor

WEAPON RETENTION

WEAPON RETENTION

There will be times in the line of duty that an Officer may face a subject who is attempting to disarm the Officer and secure their baton. Presented below are several strategies and techniques that an Officer can utilize to secure their baton while in a conflict situation. All techniques should be used only when deemed appropriate by the Officer based on the existing threat level. There will be times when the Officer feels it is safer to retain the baton, and others when it is safer to sacrifice the baton in favor of another force option, such as a firearm.

The Officer must remember that a subject attempting to gain their baton immediately creates the possibility of a lethal force situation. Officers are trained in the proper use of the baton and in their hands it can effectively be utilized as a less lethal force option tool.
A subject armed with an Officer's baton however is unlikely to be trained in proper baton methods and is likely to use the baton in a manner which would constitute lethal force. In close proximity, with means and opportunity the attempt to disarm an Officer is a clear sign of intent to harm. With means, opportunity, and intent present a dangerous scenario is created for the Officer.

IMPACT RETENTION

If an Officer finds themselves struggling to retain their baton, and deem that it is necessary to retain the baton, the Officer should use every tool available to them to maintain their weapon. Officer's can use stunning blows such as hand, elbow, knee and foot strikes to diminish the subject and retain the baton.

ONE HANDED CROSS GRAB TO THE BATON

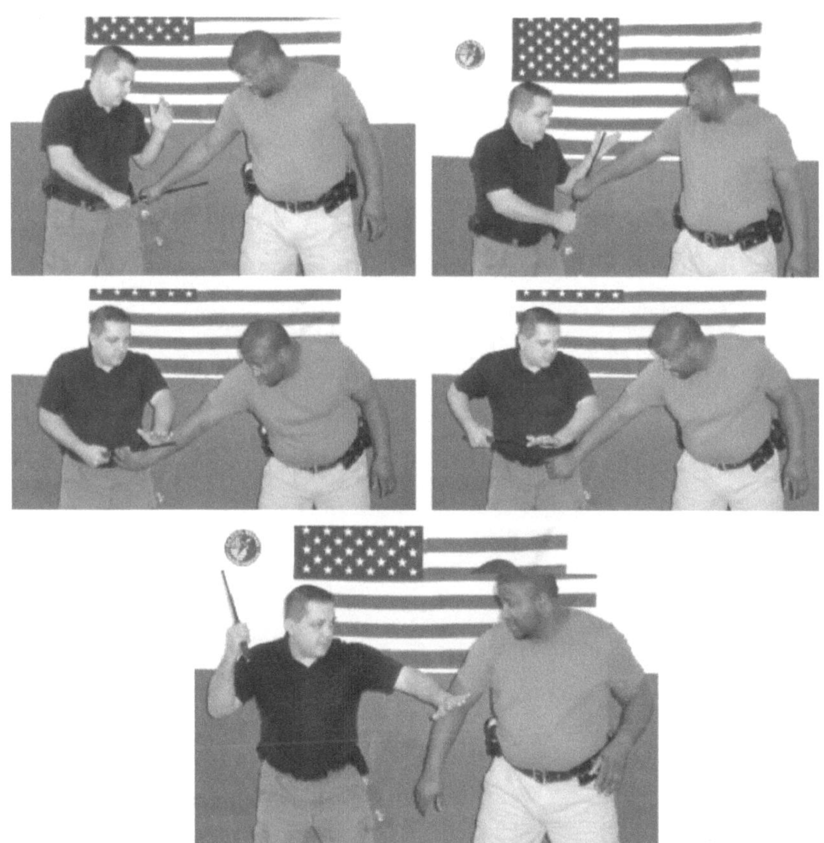

1. The subject grabs the baton.

2. The Officer then rotates the tip of the baton upwards and reinforces it with his hand.

3. The baton will now rest against the subject's hand/arm the Officer pushes down on the arm breaking the subjects grip.

4. The Officer pulls the butt of the baton backwards towards his hips forcefully.

5. The Officer steps back and assumes a conflict stance, using the Support hand to maintain distance.

SAME SIDE ONE HANDED GRAB TO THE BATON

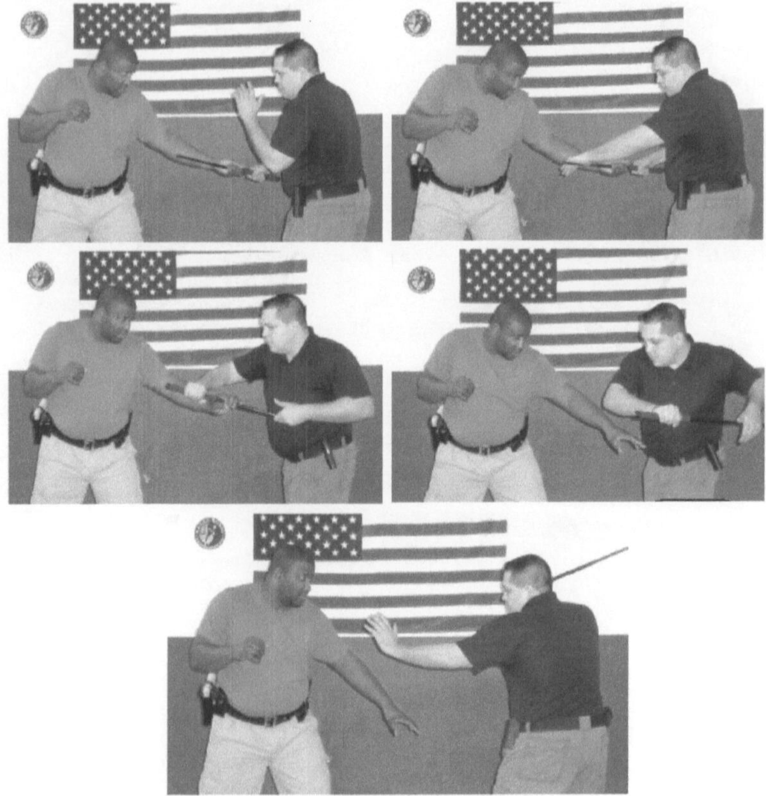

The subject grabs the baton with one hand near the end shaft and the grip. The Officer grabs the end shaft to secure a two handed grip on the baton. The Officer then rotates the grip of the baton over the subjects arm as he steps forward. The baton will now rest against the subjects extended arms; the Officer pushes down on the arm breaking the subjects grip. The Officer pulls the tip of the baton backwards towards his hips forcefully. The Officer then steps back and assumes a conflict stance, using the Support hand to maintain distance.

TWO HANDED BATON GRAB

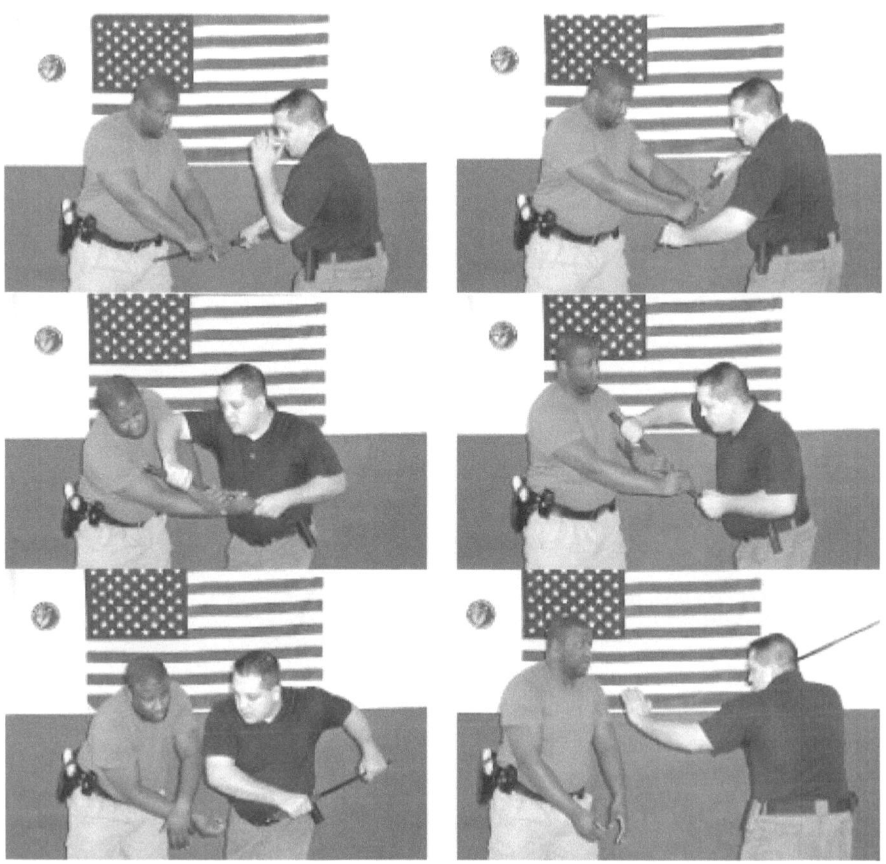

The subject grabs the baton with two hands near the end shaft and the grip. The Officer grabs the end shaft to secure a two handed grip on the baton. The Officer then rotates the grip of the baton over the subject's arms as he steps forward. The baton will now rest against the subjects extended arms; the Officer pushes down on the arms breaking the subjects grip. The Officer pulls the tip of the baton backwards towards his hips forcefully. The Officer steps back and assumes a conflict stance, using the Support hand to maintain distance.

SAME SIDE WRIST GRAB

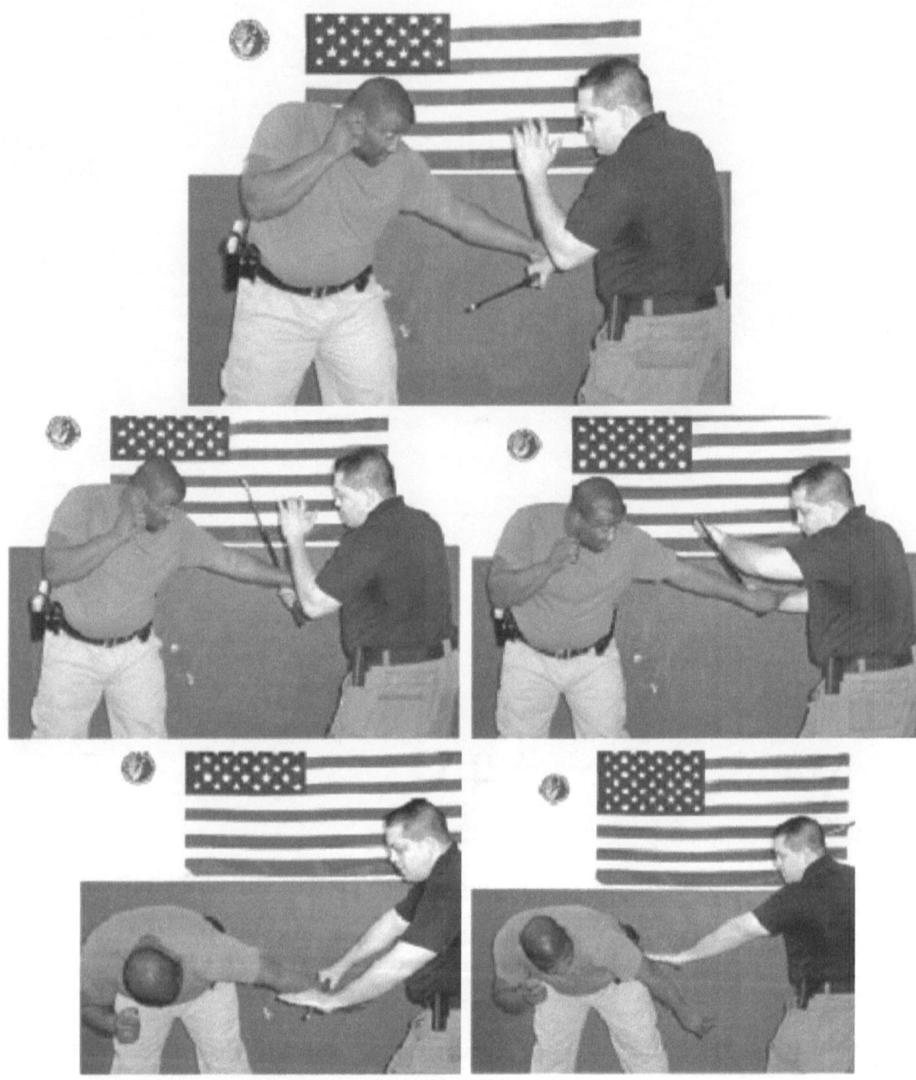

The subject grabs the Officer's wrist. The Officer then rotates the tip of the baton upwards on the outside of the subjects arm and reinforces it with his hand. The baton will now rest against the subject's hand/arm the Officer pushes down on the arm breaking the subjects grip. The Officer steps back and assumes a conflict stance, using the Support hand to maintain distance.

ONE HANDED CROSS GRAB TO THE WRIST

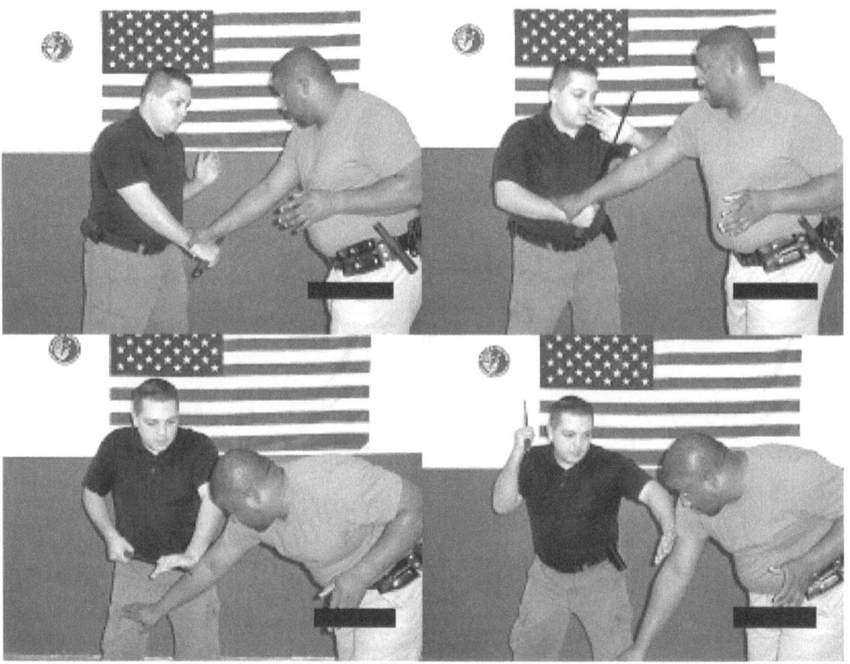

The subject grabs the baton. The Officer then rotates the tip of the baton upwards and reinforces it with his hand. The baton will now rest against the subject's hand/arm the Officer pushes down on the arm breaking the subjects grip while the Officer pulls the butt of the baton backwards towards his hips forcefully. The Officer steps back and assumes a conflict stance, using the Support hand to maintain distance.

TWO HANDED WRIST GRAB

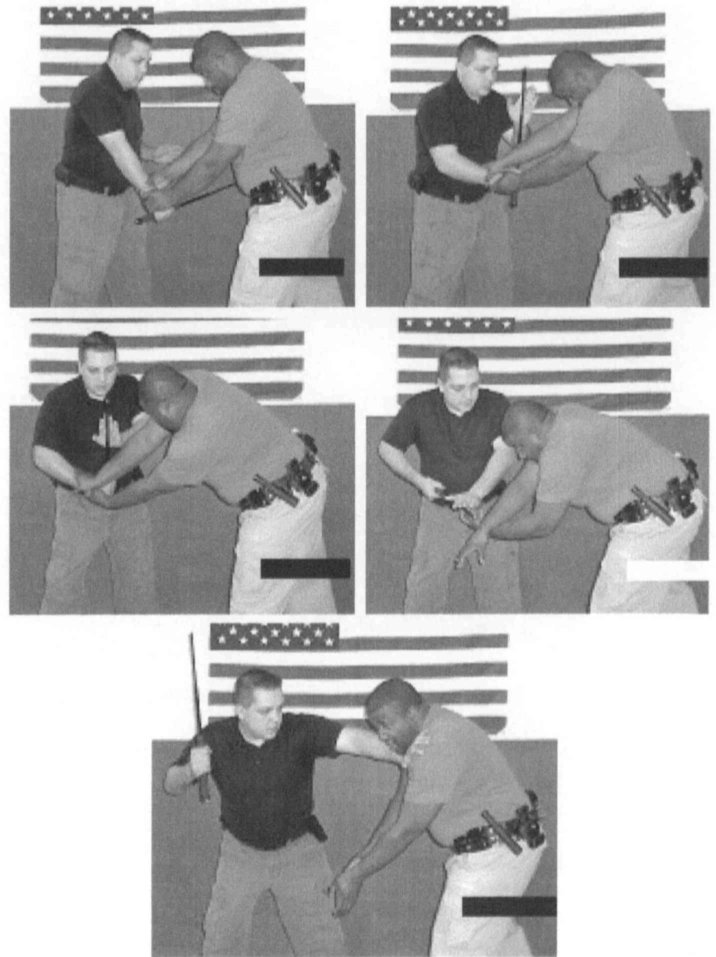

The subject grabs the Officer's wrist with two hands. The Officer then rotates the tip of the baton upwards and reinforces it with his hand. The baton will now rest against the subject's hand/arm the Officer pushes down on the arm breaking the subjects grip. The Officer pulls the butt of the baton backwards towards his hips forcefully. The Officer steps back and assumes a conflict stance, using the Support hand to maintain distance.

TWO HANDED WRIST GRAB

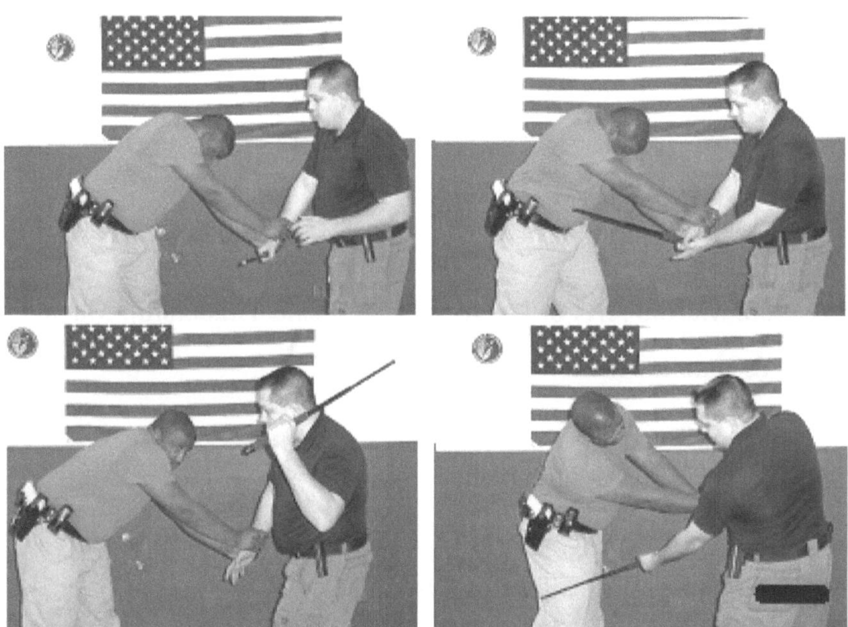

The subject grabs the Officer's wrist with two hands. The Officer quickly passes the baton to his free hand. The Officer executes a stunning blow to the subject's thigh, affecting a release.

BIBLIOGRAPHY

1. MCRP 3-02B Close Combat U.S. Marine Corps

2. FM 21-150 Combatives US Army

3. Premiere Martial Arts of Universal City Texas Leadership Manual By Tom & Juanita Howanic

4. Slash & Thrust By John Sanchez

5. Monadnock Defensive Tactics System Manual by Joseph Truncale & Terry E. Smith

6. FMFRP 12-80: Kill or Get Killed U.S. Marine Corps

7. Law Officer Magazine: Expandable Batons: What's out there & how to choose By Bob Willis

8. The Evolution of the Police Baton

9. Pro-Systems Baton Manual by Joseph Truncale

10. Cold Steel by John Styers

ABOUT THE AUTHOR

Fernan Vargas is the Founder of Raven Tactical International. He has been a student of the Martial Arts for over 30 years. In that Time Mr. Vargas has specialized in the applications of modern and historic combat arts for the purpose of self-protection. Mr. Vargas is a current safety patrol leader and trainer for the Chicago Chapter of the World famous Guardian Angels safety patrol. As a Guardian Angel, Mr. Vargas designed the official defensive tactics program for the organization. As certified law enforcement trainer Mr. Vargas has taught defensive tactics to law enforcement and security personnel at the local, state and federal level including agencies such as the Pentagon Force Protection Agency, and the Colorado and Virginia Defense Forces. Mr. Vargas has also taught military personnel and civilians in the United States and abroad in countries such as Spain, Italy and Canada. Mr. Vargas holds several instructor credentials in a variety of combat methods both modern and historical, Eastern and Western.

Mr. Vargas is the current United States representative for the Instituto Per Le Tradizioni Marziali Italiane. Mr. Vargas was granted the title of Soma De Cutel by Professor Gilberto Pauciullo, and the title of Master at Arms by Ernest Emerson and the Order of the Black Shamrock.

Mr. Vargas holds the following Impact Weapons teaching credentials:
Certified Instructor: ASP Tactical Baton
Certified Instructor: Monadnock Expandable Baton System
Certified Instructor: Police Tactical Training Tactical Baton System
Certified Instructor: Pro-Systems Police Baton System.
Certified Instructor: Pro-Systems Police Mini-Baton System.
Certified Instructor: Shinja Stick Combatives System
Menkyo Kaiden: Bushi Satori Ryu Bo-Jutsu
Instructor Certification: DFA Kali

WWW.FERNANVARGAS.COM

WWW.RAVENTACTICAL.COM

WWW.THERAVENTRIBE.COM

www.ingramcontent.com/pod-product-compliance
Ingram Content Group UK Ltd.
Pitfield, Milton Keynes, MK11 3LW, UK
UKHW041920190726
13854UKWH00003B/1351